Y0-CZO-155

THE VERY LITTLE
ANGEL

Stephanie Jeffs

Illustrated by Maria Cristina Lo Cascio

*D*o you believe in angels?

Maybe you've heard that you have a guardian angel, who watches over you and keeps you safe. Maybe you've heard that angels sometimes visit people, bringing them messages from God. Maybe you place an angel on the top of your tree when you decorate it at Christmas time.

Whatever you've heard, it's no secret! Angels really do exist. Angels are God's special messengers.

One very special night, the sky was filled with the light of many angels who had come to earth. They came to sing a beautiful song to God, because God had done something very wonderful.

This is the story about what happened on that special night. It is also the story of the part played by one very little angel.

"Finished!" sighed the very
little angel, as she threw down
her duster.

She looked at the French horn.
It was gold and gleaming, and it
shone as it caught the bright light
of heaven. It looked beautiful.
Everything looked beautiful in heaven.

The very little angel started to
polish the golden surface of a harp
with her cloth. She saw her reflection.
One day she wouldn't be a little
angel anymore.

She would be a big angel, a
proper angel, a grown-up angel.
She couldn't wait!

The sound of the trumpet made the little angel jump. She leaped into the air. There were angels everywhere!

Some were big, and some were strong; but all were very beautiful.

They stood in rows and chattered excitedly to one another.

"What's happening?" wondered the very little angel, as she took her place at the end of the line. Everyone became silent.

The Chief Angel held up the scroll for everyone to see. He broke the seal and slowly unrolled it. Nobody moved.

The very little angel could hardly breathe.

"Angels!" said the Chief Angel. "I have some exciting news!

"Today, one of us will go to earth to deliver a very special message from God."

The very little angel gasped and clapped her hands.

She didn't notice the other angels as they turned to look at her.

11

The Chief Angel continued. "God has chosen a young girl named Mary to do something very special. I need an angel who is prepared to do something very special for God."

The Chief Angel paused, and the heavens fell silent.

The very little angel's wings quivered with excitement. She would do anything to please God. She already polished and dusted for God. She sang and danced for God. Perhaps this was her chance to deliver a message for God. Then she would be a proper, grown-up angel.

"I will!" said the very little angel to herself. "I will deliver God's special message!"

She took a deep breath.

"Gabriel!" The Chief
Angel's voice boomed
through the company.
"Gabriel will take God's
message to earth."

14

The angels started to cheer and clap.
Gabriel stepped forward and took the
scroll in his hand.

The very little angel felt her eyes
prickle with tears. She brushed them
away. Without looking up, she tried to
clap with the others.

The multitude of angels swarmed around Gabriel. They flew with him as he dove from the bright light of heaven into the darkness outside. Then they hovered in the air, waiting for him to return.

The very little angel fluttered on tiptoes, but she was just too little to see.

"Glory to God!" she sang. "Glory to God in the highest and peace to God's people on earth!"

She looked around and saw that all the other angels were singing the same song. She had never heard it before, but it came from deep within her. She looked at the other angels shining in the darkness and knew that she must be shining too.

It was then that the little angel realized for the first time that it didn't matter that she was a very little angel. She knew that God had given her this very special task, and it would be the most important thing that she would ever do. God had sent Jesus to be the Savior of the world! What a wonderful God!

And the very little angel knew that what Gabriel had told her was true. Jesus was born, and nothing would ever be the same.

"Glory to God!" she sang again and again. "Glory to God in the highest and peace to God's people on earth!"

"Don't be afraid!" she heard him shout. "I am here with good news for you!"

Suddenly the angels filled the night sky with light.

The very little angel saw for the first time a group of men huddled together on a hillside. She saw their frightened faces and wanted to tell them not to be afraid.

She saw the brightest of all stars shining in the darkness. In a small stable she could see a young woman holding a tiny baby. She knew that this was Mary with Jesus, God's only Son.

Without warning, the trumpet
sounded and all of heaven stood
still. Gabriel clasped the very little angel
by the hand and led her, along with
every other angel, out towards the edge
of the night.

"Jesus is part of God's plan to save the world. Once he is born, nothing will ever be the same. Every angel will be needed to sing and dance, because of the wonderful thing God has done! Are you ready to join us, little angel?" asked Gabriel.

The very little angel thought for a moment. Then she nodded and her face broke into an enormous smile. Then her smile changed into a giggle and became a laugh. She had never felt so happy!

Published in the United States of America by
Abingdon Press, 201 Eighth Avenue South, Nashville, Tennessee 37202
ISBN 978-0-687-648238
First edition 2008

Copyright © 2008 Anno Domini Publishing
1 Churchgates, The Wilderness, Berkhamsted, Herts HP4 2UB
Text copyright © 2008 Stephanie Jeffs
Illustrations copyright © 2008 Maria Cristina Lo Cascio

Publishing Director Annette Reynolds
Editor Nicola Bull
Art Director Gerald Rogers
Pre-production Krystyna Kowalska Hewitt
Production John Laister

Printed and bound in Singapore